RIPLEY KOOL
AND THE INVESTIGATORS

The Parrot Squawks at Midnight

THOMAS LOCKHAVEN

TWISTED KEY
publishing

2024

First Printing: 2026

ISBN 978-1-63911-207-4

Twisted Key Publishing, LLC
www.twistedkeypublishing.com

Table of Contents

Chapter 1

"Those ruffians! They kidnapped Thaddeus!" The older woman shook a bony fist.

"And Thaddeus is your…?" Gilly made a rolling motion with her hand, gently encouraging Mrs. Cornthumper to continue.

"Brother. Cat. Dog. Neighbor. Son," Ripley began churning out names like a raisin in a raisin factory.

"Parrot!" exclaimed Mrs. Cornthumper contemptuously. "Thaddeus is my *best* friend and a *talented* karaoke partner."

"Mhm, karaoke," Gilly mouthed, scribbling into her notepad in an attempt to appear engaged. In reality, she was drawing a pony in a field of daisies. She adored ponies.

"You should have heard us harmonize…" Mrs. Cornthumper reminisced, a carefree smile crossing her face. "My big microphone, his tiny microphone. He'd hold it in his little claw like this." She curled her hand into a tiny fist as if holding a tiny microphone. "It was magical." She said *magical* like you would say *jazz hands!*

"I'm sure," Ripley acknowledged. "You wouldn't happen to have a recent picture of Thaddeus, would you?"

"Of course," Mrs. Cornthumper gestured to a framed photo on the kitchen counter. Mrs. Cornthumper wore a silver sequined over-the-shoulder number in the photograph; her hair looked like a stack of fluffy clouds atop her head. It was so tall that it continued off that picture and had to be shown in another picture. Thaddeus looked equally fetching, dressed in his handsome, tiny tuxedo and top hat, a miniature golden microphone in his claw. All he was missing was a monocle.

"I'm sure he was *quite* the crooner," said Alexis diplomatically as she rummaged through Mrs. C's refrigerator.

"Yes," agreed Mrs. Cornthumper, staring

longingly at the photo. She looked up, noticed Alexis's backside poking out of her refrigerator, and declared, "What are you doing?" Her voice rang out like a bell.

The older woman placed her hands on her hips and scrunched up her face, staring at Alexis. Ripley errantly misread the situation; he'd just put his hands on his hips and began to swivel when he realized his mistake. His shoulders sagged. You see, Ripley was a master of the Macarena. However, truth be told, he preferred the *salsa*… with chips and dip. Ba-ding-bop.

"I was merely investigating. Sometimes *ancient* people such as yourself—" Alexis began explaining only to be smacked in the back of the head by Gilly.

"You can't say that," Gilly berated her.

"I apologize," said Alexis. "I didn't mean to offend you. Occasionally, old-*er* people will *mistakenly* put their pets in the fridge. Sometimes it's a cat or a bird—"

"Or fish," interjected Ripley, feeling left out. He was a fan of lists, alphabetizing, and bullet points. He abhorred visual arrangers, people that organized by color—*so annoying!*

"Their pet will hop or fly into a fridge, *undetected*," Alexis made air quotes, "next thing you know, you're feasting on a frozen—"

"Okay, okay, okay." Gilly jumped in and waved her hands in the air as if magically erasing what Alexis had said.

"By the way," Alexis inquired, turning her attention back to the fridge, "while the door is open, are you going to eat those grapes?" She tapped the crisper drawer with her black high-top Converse.

"Get *out* of my refrigerator," demanded Mrs. Cornthumper. "Now!"

"Sheesh, forgive me for doing a little investigating."

"Those grapes are for Thaddeus," hissed Mrs. Cornthumper. "You three are *exasperating*," she seethed.

"Thank you, ma'am," Ripley nodded ingratiatingly.

Mrs. Cornthumper took in a deep, slow breath, sucking it threw her front teeth like the posh British folk sip tea.

"Listen, I seem to have made a serious mistake hiring you." She waved a bony finger, silencing Gilly who was about to speak. "I think I'll just hire the Sorespoon Detective Group; they have five stars on Yelp and an English Spaniel who is supposed to be able to detect ghosts and evil spirits."

"Ha! *Sorespoon*?" Alexis nearly choked on a muffin. Gilly's eyes narrowed; she gave Alexis a where-did-you-get-that-muffin look.

"Mrs. Cornthumper," Gilly said, mimicking a voice from a serious woman lawyer she'd seen on television. "We take investigating *very* seriously." Alexis and Ripley nodded in agreement. "Tell me, do you want your beloved Thaddeus back, or are you ready for a *solo* career in karaoke?"

"I'm *sure* that the Sorespoon agency could—"

"Could," said Alexis, jumping on the word as she spread a dollop of jelly across her muffin. "Do you want someone who *could* get your parrot back?" She shoved the last bite of muffin into her mouth and wiped her mouth on Mrs. Cornthumper's dishcloth. "Because we *will* get Thaddeus back." Gilly and Ripley nodded in agreement. "You don't look like someone who leaves important matters to chance," Alexis proclaimed through a mouthful of muffin.

"Well, I…," Mrs. Cornthumper waffled.

"I agree with Alexis," Gilly jumped in. "We have a proven track record." She suddenly stopped and looked Mrs. Cornthumper dead in the eye. "However, I don't think you are being upfront with us; this isn't just about a missing parrot—there's more." Gilly crossed her arms.

"Well…," Mrs. Cornthumper sighed, "I guess there's no harm letting you in on our little secret."

Chapter 2

"When I first met my late husband, Cornelius, I instantly fell in love with him. He was such a kind soul, and so…"

"Handsome," Alexis jumped in.

"Whimsical," suggested Gilly.

"Adroit," Ripley shouted.

"Ah, *unassuming*," Alexis smiled and nodded slowly, as if she'd known all along.

"Adventurous," smiled Mrs. Cornthumper.

"Sounds like a *wonderful* man," said Alexis, dipping a cookie into a glass of milk.

"He was. Cornelius loved mysteries and puzzles; life was always an adventure with him."

Ripley shifted uncomfortably; all this emotional stuff was making him a bit queasy like the time he drank chunky milk. "So, you said there was more to the story? Skipping the romance bit."

"Hold your horses; I'm getting there," fussed Mrs. Cornthumper. Gilly shot Ripley a look. "Your generation, always in a hurry, you need to paint a picture—a little backstory for context."

"Please," Ripley smiled apologetically, "take your time."

"Ahem," Mrs. Cornthumper cleared her throat. "Cornelius raised Thaddeus from the time he was nothing but a tiny little egg. When his little beak poked through that shell… well, those two were inseparable. Everywhere Cornelius went, Thaddeus followed him."

Gilly and Alexis looked at each other, sharing an *awe* moment. Ripley rolled his eyes in disgust.

"I love romantic stories," said Alexis between mouthfuls of banana.

"I'm sorry," Mrs. Cornthumper arched an eyebrow at Alexis. "Do your parents *not*

feed you?"

"She eats when she's thinking," explained Gilly. "I once saw her eat an entire wheel of cheese."

"Where there's a wheel, there's a way," said Ripley.

"It's true," Alexis nodded. "I gained twelve pounds in one day. But the *thoughts* I had," she shook her head as if she couldn't believe it herself. "Honestly," she gestured with the half-eaten banana, "if I had out-of-control curly white hair, people would have mistaken me for Albert Einstein."

"Except for the fact that he was a man… and he's deceased," said Gilly poignantly.

"R.I.P.," whispered Ripley solemnly.

"I'm sorry, Mrs. Cornthumper," said Gilly, giving her an apologetic smile. "You were telling us about your husband."

"About a month before he passed, he told me that he was close to finding something that would *enrich* our lives forever."

"Treasure," mouthed Alexis.

"No, deodorant," Ripley shook his head. "Of course, it's treasure. It *is* treasure, isn't it?"

"No matter how many times I asked him, he wouldn't divulge his secret."

"But you, of course, knew what it was," he gave Mrs. Cornthumper a sly smile.

She nodded her head and smiled. All was silent for a moment except for the whir of the garbage disposal. "Sorry," whispered Alexis.

"So, what was it? I was right, right?" Ripley let the question hang in the air.

"I *suspect* that he found the Viento Dorado," said Mrs. Cornthumper.

"The Italian singer?" gasped Ripley.

"No," Mrs. Cornthumper gave him a confused look. "The Viento Dorado was a Spanish trade ship that sank off the coast of Massachusetts in a storm. There was said to have been half a ton of Spanish coins in its cargo hold."

"And you think he found the Viento Dorito?" asked Alexis.

"The Viento Dorado. Yes, he'd been searching for twenty-five years for that shipwreck," said Mrs. Cornthumper; she couldn't help but smile. "I think he found it."

Gilly closed her eyes. "Half a ton, that's gotta be worth millions!"

Ripley released a slow whistle. "Did you say millions as in millions?"

Gilly nodded her head, "As in a one, followed by six zeroes."

"I see," said Ripley. "Mrs. Cornthumper, I was wondering if you'd be willing to renegotiate our contract?"

"I'm confused," said Alexis. "How does Thaddeus fit into all of this? You said he went wherever your husband went. Do you think he knows where the treasure is, and whoever stole him is trying to get him to talk?"

"It's too horrible to think about," Mrs. Cornthumper shook her hands. "I hate the thought of poor Thaddeus being poked and prodded for information."

Ripley imagined Thaddeus wearing a

blindfold, tied to a chair, a bright light in his face, being jabbed in the chest with a finger. She was right; it was terrifying.

"So," said Gilly softly, "Thaddeus was taken because he may know where the gold is?"

"Yes. Remember that I told you Cornelius loved puzzles and mysteries?" The children nodded in unison. "Well, it had been about a month since he had passed, and I was packing up some of his things from his desk when I saw the corner of an envelope poking out from beneath his desk blotter."

"Desk blotter?" asked Alexis.

"It's like a place mat for your desk. It protects the surface of your desk," explained Gilly.

"Gotcha," nodded Alexis. "Sorry for interrupting."

"It's fine, dear," she waved her apology aside. "I pulled out the envelope… it was in the shape of a heart," Mrs. Cornthumper's voice sounded delicate, like a feather-thin glass bell that would shatter if rang. She took a quavering breath, dabbed at her eyes, then continued. "I opened the envelope, and inside was a card, and inside the card, a puzzle from my dear Cornelius."

Alexis grabbed a napkin from the kitchen counter and handed it to Mrs. Cornthumper, who blew her nose like a trumpet. Perhaps in her past life, she had been an elephant.

"Thank you," she smiled at Alexis.

Ripley edged the trash can toward Mrs. Cornthumper and pressed the pedal with his foot, opening the lid. He wasn't keen on snot or eye boogers. The only liquids acceptable from a person's face were sweat and tears, but not at the same time... because that was just confusing.

Mrs. Cornthumper tossed the napkin into the trash, and Ripley let the lid close with a *thump*. "Where was I?" she asked.

From the weight of that napkin, I'd say dehydrated, thought Ripley.

"You've been in the kitchen the whole time," said Alexis helpfully.

"Cornelius... you said he left you a puzzle," Gilly reminded her.

"Oh yes. The card said that he'd found the treasure. I could *only* assume that he meant the Viento Dorado. He went on to say that I would have to figure out the cipher key….” She looked at the children expectantly.

“Of course,” said Ripley excitedly, “you needed the cipher key to break the code. And let me guess, Thaddeus knows what it is.”

“Exactly,” nodded Mrs. Cornthumper. “The letter said in order to figure out the cipher key, I would have to tell Thaddeus the name of the first song Cornelius and I danced to, and he’ll respond with the key.”

“That’s so cool,” said Alexis.

“I’m sorry,” Gilly looked confused. “Why didn’t you ask Thaddeus immediately?”

“Because,” Mrs. Cornthumper frowned, “I’m ashamed to say, but I have no recollection of the song. All I remember about the dance is being lost in those big brown eyes."

"Ugh," Ripley let the back of his head fall back against the wall. "*Gross*."

A clever look passed over Gilly's face, "I think I have an idea how to solve that problem. But first things first, how did anyone else find out about the letter and the treasure?"

"Well," Mrs. Cornthumper frowned and shook her head, "it was my fault."

Chapter 3

"I was so excited when I found the card…
I was about to burst."

"I bet," Gilly exclaimed, "hard to keep a
secret like that!"

"I went to Helen's, a little restaurant off of
Main, to meet with my book friends for
breakfast. We meet there every
Thursday," Mrs. Cornthumper explained.
"I told them the whole story. Of course,
they feigned excitement; I could tell that
they thought I was being foolish."

"Even though Cornelius had found other
treasures?" asked Alexis.

"You have to realize the other treasures
were nothing compared to this. Coins,
swords, and other artifacts worth
thousands of dollars, mind you. But the
Viento Dorado is well known in the realm
of treasure hunters—they've searched for

it for hundreds of years."

"I can imagine they would be a little dubious," Gilly nodded. "What happened next?"

"I showed them the card as proof. They passed it around the table. I'm not sure it really convinced them, but then the waitress appeared with hot coffee and a steaming pile of plates balanced on her arm, and I got distracted."

"Understandable," said Alexis. "There was a lot going on."

"Yes," Mrs. Cornthumper smiled appreciatively at Alexis's attempt to make her feel better. "I remember placing the card on the seat next to me, but in all the chaos, it must have gotten knocked onto the floor. It wasn't until I was pulling into the driveway that I realized I'd left the card. I called immediately, but—" her voice trailed off.

"I'm sorry, Mrs. Cornthumper," said Ripley. "That's how they knew Thaddeus could reveal the cipher."

"Yes, a horrible mistake, and now Thaddeus is in danger. I'm so disappointed in myself."

"Do you think it was someone from your book club?" asked Alexis.

"Oh no, never; I've known these girls since primary school. They would *never* do such a thing."

"Well, it had to be someone you knew… or Cornelius knew." Mrs. Cornthumper gave Ripley a questioning look. "Because they knew who Thaddeus was and where you live. They may have even overheard you at the diner."

"Well, Thaddeus is very well known, especially in karaoke circles. His Elvis impersonation was top-notch."

"I'm sure," said Gilly supportively.

"Thaddeus is very social; we keep his cage in front of the picture window in the living room. He likes to say hello to the neighbors as they pass by. Everyone knows him."

"Thaddeus has more of a social life than I do," moaned Ripley.

"A rock has more of a social life than you," said Alexis.

"May we see your dining room?" asked Gilly.

"Of course." Mrs. Cornthumper led them out of the kitchen into a narrow hallway. Pictures of Thaddeus dressed in numerous costumes lined the walls: Thaddeus as a Viking, scarecrow, fireman, construction worker, sailor, and Elvis, complete with sideburns and sequined pants.

"He's got quite an extensive wardrobe," said Gilly, pointing to a picture of Thaddeus sporting a hoodie, gold chain, and sunglasses.

"Cornelius dressed him up every day. That picture," she gestured to the one Gilly had pointed out, "was in his *rap* and *hip-hop* days. He'd sing, drop the microphone, and then fold his wings across his chest."

"Impressive," nodded Ripley, jutting out his lower jaw. "What about this one, where he's in the sailor outfit? Is that your boat?"

"Yes," nodded Mrs. Cornthumper. "Pieces of Eight. We traveled thousands of miles over the past fifty years: the Atlantic Ocean, Pacific, Mediterranean. So many memories."

"Why Pieces of Eight?" asked Ripley.

"Cornelius was a big fan of Robert Stevenson's book *Treasure Island*—"

"Oh, we had to read that book in English," Gilly interrupted.

"Then you'll remember Long John Silver's

parrot constantly saying, 'Pieces of eight! Pieces of eight!'"

"Because he was reminding them about the pirate's treasure," Gilly recalled.

"That's right. It was a Spanish coin marked with the number eight. So Cornelius, forever the adventurer, christened our boat, *Pieces of Eight*."

"Cool," said Ripley. He followed the others as Mrs. Cornthumper led them into the dining room—a small, charming mint-green room with white baseboards. An oval table sat in the center, a basket of decorative fruit atop. A chandelier hung from the ceiling, and on the far side of the room, a giant picture window took up the entire wall.

"Wow," said Gilly, peering through the window, "Thaddeus had a spectacular view."

"Oh yes, this was one of his favorite spots. As I said, he loves talking to the neighbors and squawking at the other birds and squirrels."

"So," said Ripley, exploring the extended windowsill where the outline of Thaddeus's cage was still apparent, "they stole his cage as well?"

"It's the only way they could have taken him. He's a blue and gold macaw. His claws can tear bark off a tree as easily as you can tear open a candy wrapper, and his beak is strong enough to severely injure you."

"Forget a guard dog," said Ripley. "Just buy a parrot."

"I read that they can crack open a walnut shell…" said Gilly. "Imagine what they could do to your finger."

"Eh… I'd rather not," said Ripley, glancing

down at his hand.

"What's that?" asked Gilly, pointing at Ripley's foot.

"What's what?" Ripley took a step back.

"By your shoe, it looks like—"

Ripley knelt. "It's a piece of blue latex," he said, picking it up from the floor, "like from a latex glove."

"Makes sense," nodded Alexis through a series of *crunch crunches*, "the thief didn't want to leave fingerprints."

Gilly joined him by the window and examined the outline left from the cage on the extended windowsill. "They had to take his cage," said Mrs. Cornthumper. "No one except Cornelius and I could handle Thaddeus."

Crunch. Crunch. "Would you mind asking your neighbors if they saw anything?" asked Alexis. "An unfamiliar car in your driveway, perhaps?"

 "Yes, of course, I'll ask. If there is anything I can do to help, just let me know."

"Alright," Alexis said, "we should probably get going. Oh, and by the way, Mrs. Cornthumper, your granola is a bit stale."

"That's potpourri, dear."

"Okay, fair enough. Your potpourri is quite stale," Alexis replied matter-of-factly.

Gilly inhaled, inflated her cheeks, and released the air in a slow show of disappointment. "Don't worry," she assured Mrs. Cornthumper, "we're much better at solving crimes than…" she looked at Ripley, struggling to find the right word.

"Existing?" offered Alexis.

"Don't worry, we'll figure it out," Ripley gave Mrs. Cornthumper a confident smile. "We *always* do."

Alexis placed the bowl back on the table, and a ring of potpourri circled her lips.

She grabbed an orange from the wooden bowl atop the dining room table. "One for the road," she declared, tossing it in the air.

Mrs. Cornthumper didn't have the heart to tell her it was plastic.

Chapter 4

Ripley slid his sunglasses onto his nose. "So, whoever took Thaddeus had to know Cornelius."

"Sounds right," agreed Gilly. "They knew Thaddeus was a parrot, not a person, and they knew where to find him."

"Not to mention the fact that they believed Cornelius's story about finding the treasure," added Alexis.

"I say we start at the marina where he keeps his boat. If he found the treasure, maybe it's hidden there," said Gilly.

"Or someone saw him bring it ashore," offered Ripley.

"Either way, we should start at the marina," said Gilly.

The three sleuths hopped on their bikes and pedaled through Mrs. Cornthumper's neighborhood. Sprinklers chattered, birds fluttered, and bees buzzed from colorful flowers beneath the golden sunlight. Ripley closed his eyes and breathed deeply as they cruised down Knoxwood Hill, the warm breeze filling his lungs.

To their right, golfers dressed in pastel shorts and knit shirts rode around in golf carts at the Driftwood Country Club. The trio turned onto Seashore Drive, traveling single file along the narrow two-lane road. They nosed their bikes into the Riverscape Marina parking lot and wheeled them into a rack alongside a weathered statue of Edmond Tipps, the generous benefactor who had donated the land for the marina.

"Do you smell that? The sweet nectar of the gods filleth the air," Alexis declared. She pointed to the Sandbar Restaurant, her *favorite* place to eat. The food was top-notch and boasted an all-you-can-eat special every night. Wednesday, in particular, held a special place in Alexis's heart, featuring endless amounts of popcorn shrimp and hushpuppies.

A gust of wind blew, carrying metallic pings as sailboat rigging clinked and clanged against masts. Seagulls perched along the dock railings, waiting for scraps from incoming fishing boats.

"Either of you have a clue where his boat might be docked?" asked Ripley, scanning the myriad of boats bobbing in the water alongside the massive docks. "There's like hundreds of them."

"Wait here, I'll run and ask the harbor master. I'm sure they'll know." Alexis darted off before Gilly or Ripley could reply.

"Might as well look around while she checks—"

"Or," suggested Gilly, pulling out her phone, "I can use this handy device and ask Mrs. Cornthumper where the boat's located."

"Eh, that makes too much sense," Ripley smiled.

Gilly tapped her screen; Mrs. Cornthumper picked up after three rings. She put the call on speaker so Ripley could hear.

"Hi, Mrs. Cornthumper, it's Gilly. I'm sorry to bother you so soon—"

"Not a bother at all, dear, what is it?"

"We're at the Riverscape Marina, and we sort of underestimated how many boats there would be."

"Oh, I see," said Mrs. Cornthumper, quickly catching on. "You have no idea where to find his boat."

"No, ma'am."

"It's dock four, slip eight, dear."

"Thank you so much," Gilly smiled reflexively. "We want to do a bit of investigating and figured the marina would be the best place to start."

"You'll need a key, dear, to get inside the

cabin. Cornelius kept everything locked up tighter than a drum. I'm running out to the pharmacy; I'll swing by and drop off the key."

"Okay, we'll meet you at his boat."

"I'll be there in ten minutes," said Mrs. Cornthumper, ending the call.

"Harbor master's not there," mumbled a familiar voice behind Ripley and Gilly.

"I see you had no problem locating food," smirked Ripley. Alexis held a half-eaten hot dog in one hand and a red and white cardboard container overflowing with tater tots.

"Don't be rude," Alexis frowned. "I got you a hot dog too."

Ripley looked at her expectantly, "I don't see it… oh… let me guess."

"I may have eaten it," Alexis admitted. "What? It was a long walk… and where is she off to?" she asked between chomps.

"Awe man. Cornelius's boat, come on."

They went from speedwalking to a slow jog in an effort to catch Gilly, who Ripley suspected was secretly training for Olympic speedwalking. All she needed was the cushy shoes older people wore.

"If she goes any faster, her sneakers are going to ignite," said Alexis, balancing her tower of hushpuppies. She paused midstride, grabbing Ripley's shoulder with a ketchupy hand.

"Eesh, for real?" Ripley shrugged his shoulder away. "I just washed this shirt."

"Sorry, but I don't think we're alone." Alexis looked over her shoulder, "I've got this feeling…" she said nervously.

"Is it gas? Maybe a change in diet? Perhaps save some carbs for the rest of the world."

"No," she punched his shoulder. "For real! Don't you ever get that feeling like someone's watching you?"

"Please," Ripley lowered his sunglasses. "With these cheekbones, everyone is watching me."

"Your modesty is inspiring."

"Alexis, no one is watching us; we're *kids*

on a dock. No one cares, believe me," Ripley reassured her.

"I see the boat," Gilly yelled over her shoulder.

"That's like saying, 'I see water,'" Ripley called out. "If you haven't noticed, we're surrounded by boats."

Gilly came to a stop, hands on hips, a satisfied look on her face. "Does the water say *Pieces of Eight*?"

"No," said Ripley, joining her. "But it waves."

"Are you *shore*," laughed Alexis.

"Sea for yourself," joked Ripley.

"You two give me legit shivers. Can you get physically ill from bad jokes? I mean, look," Gilly held out her arms. "I literally have goosebumps, your jokes are so lame."

"Sorry," whispered Ripley, "I didn't do it on

porpoise."

A strange sensation crept up Alexis's spine, like fingers crawling up her back. She spun around, but no one was there— just a row of seagulls basking in the sun, oblivious to the annoying humans. "Were they there before?"

"What?" Ripley asked, confused by her question. "The seagulls? They're everywhere."

Alexis gave them a wary look and mollified her uneasiness with a tater tot.

Cornelius's boat was impressive, stretching at least twenty-five feet from bow to stern. The hull was sky blue with white trim work. Silver railings gleamed in the sunlight. It gently rocked in the water, secured snugly to the dock by two thick ropes.

"Man, that thing has gotta be *so* fast," said Ripley, pointing to the three engines.

"It's a beautiful boat," Gilly agreed. "I say we check it out."

"Can we just get on?" Ripley turned and surveyed the marina; it was still practically empty.

"I don't see why not," said Alexis, popping a hushpuppy in her mouth. "Didn't Mrs. Cornthumper give us permission?"

"Yeah, she said we'd need the key for the

cabin, but I don't see any harm in poking around." Gilly grabbed the sun-warmed railing and hoisted herself aboard. Ripley followed behind her.

Alexis had one foot on the boat and one on the dock when she was attacked. A bloodcurdling scream rang out, followed by a heavy *thunk* as Alexis fell onto the dock.

Chapter 5

Ripley and Gilly watched in horror. For a moment, there were only feathers, beaks, legs, and arms. And then, as suddenly as it happened, the flock of saboteurs flew away, squawking in victory.

There wasn't a scrap of food left. They'd even taken Alexis's red and white checkered box. The only visible sign that they had been there at all was a dollop of bird poo on her forehead.

"That was humbling," whispered Ripley.

"An intervention of sorts," Gilly replied.

"Uh, Alexis… you've got a little something right here."

"So humiliating," Alexis burst out. She crawled to an outdoor shower, turned on the lower faucet, and washed her face. If this was a sign as to how the investigation was going to go, they were in trouble.

"Not a word," Alexis warned as Gilly held out her hand and helped her aboard. They both turned when they heard Ripley's low whistle.

"Uhm, guys, I don't think we're going to need a key." He gestured to the storage containers; they had all been pried open. Gilly noticed all of the seat cushions had been slit open as well.

"They're searching for the treasure," said Alexis.

"Or they just really hate cushions," said Ripley. He hurried to the helm; the captain's chair had been sliced open, and something had been ripped from the main console—a bouquet of colorful wires poked out of a rectangular hole.

"Why would anyone do this?" Alexis moaned.

"What is it?" asked Gilly.

Alexis nodded toward a pack of peanut butter cookies below the console that had been crushed, most likely by the thief's destruction. "They crushed a perfectly good package of cookies."

"Hey, at least they left a clue." Ripley pointed at an oily shoeprint.

"Oh yeah, totally," nodded Alexis, "that's what I meant."

"Great find, Lex!" Gilly fished out her phone and took several pictures. She laid a pencil alongside the track to help show the size of the shoeprint.

"Hey! What are you kids doing?" barked an angry male voice.

Ripley startled, hitting his head on the ceiling. He and the others scurried out of the helm like roaches from beneath an upturned box. Ripley rubbed the top of his head as he and the others made their way toward the bow of the boat.

An absurdly large man with an equally large scowl stared angrily at the sleuths. He crossed his muscular arms across his barrel chest.

Ripley thought he looked like a genie, but he was quite sure he wasn't there to grant them three wishes.

"What are you doing?" he growled. "This

is private property."

"It's okay," Gilly explained. "We're here on behalf of Mrs. Cornthumper."

"Gladys didn't say anything about having guests."

"I assure you that we were invited," Gilly said in her most serious voice, reserved for serious situations such as this.

Ripley was happy Gilly had stepped in because he was about to go with the line that he and Mrs. Cornthumper were on the same bowling league.

Captain Angry Pants seemed to contemplate what they said for a moment, and then with tremendous agility, he launched himself off the dock, over the boat's railing, landing softly like a very, very, very large cat. His jaw dropped when he saw the ripped cushions and broken storage bins. "What did you do to Cornelius's boat?"

"Woah, woah, woah," Ripley held his hands out. "We did *not* do this! We just got here."

The man stepped toward the trio and thrust a menacing finger at them. "Trespassing. Destruction of private property. I'm going to call the police!" He let his beady eyes settle on each child. "You'll never see daylight again!"

"You'll do *no* such thing, Otis," a shrill voice cried out.

"Mrs. Cornthumper!" the three teens cried out in unison.

The top-heavy man whirled around. Even though he was immense, Mrs. Cornthumper appeared to tower over him.

"Good afternoon, Gladys," he dipped his head slightly. "I just found these miscreants on your boat. Look what they've done."

"My word, Otis, don't be ridiculous, they're my guests." He reached out a hand and helped her aboard. Her eyes widened in shock. "Oh my," her hand flew to her mouth. "What happened?"

"I told you these—"

"Otis," Mrs. Cornthumper said sharply, "you and I both know that they didn't do this." Otis looked like he was about to speak but thought better of it.

"There's something you need to see in the helm," said Ripley. Mrs. Cornthumper followed him to the doorway. He stood aside and pointed to the gaping hole in the console filled with colorful wires.

"The GPS system," she gasped.

"Why would they? Oh…," Ripley turned to Mrs. Cornthumper, "they wanted the coordinates to where he'd found the treasure."

A sad look fell across Mrs. Cornthumper's face. "They have Thaddeus… the coordinates, and now, they might have the treasure."

Chapter 6

Aaaahhheeeaahhhh!

Aaaahhheeeaahhhh! Gilly's Tarzan ringtone woke her from her daydream. She grabbed her phone; the screen read, 'Mrs. C.'s video call.' Gilly patted her hair, brushed her bangs from her face, and pressed the accept button.

"Hello, Mrs. Cornthumper, how are you?" Gilly blinked her eyes and shook her head, loosening the cobwebs.

"I have news," she said excitedly. Mrs. Cornthumper obviously was new to video calling as all Gilly could see was her right nostril and the top of her lips.

"What is it?" Gilly asked the nostril.

"Well, I went door to door and asked my neighbors if they'd seen anything strange, and I found something *very* exciting." Mrs. Cornthumper's nostril flared. "Judy, Judy Lilac, said that she saw a white van parked near my house when she took Linus for a walk."

"Oh, a van, how nefarious. It could definitely be something," said Gilly.

"Judy said she didn't think too much about it until I told her Thaddeus was missing. That's when she said *this* had blown out of the van window as it pulled away." There was a blur of movement, the nostril was replaced by a bright blue feather.

"Is that a—"

"Parrot feather!" exclaimed Mrs. Cornthumper.

"Oh! Did Mrs. Lilac happen to get a license plate number or see the person driving the van?" asked Gilly excitedly.

"She didn't get a license plate number, but she did remember there was an odd slogan written on the back of the van. Something like, *Your junk is our treasure*."

"Interesting," Gilly nodded. "A+ detective work, Mrs. Cornthumper. Any chance she got a description of the driver?"

"No, I'm afraid not."

"You did a great job! Let me know if you find out anything else." They said their goodbyes and ended the video call.

Gilly opened her group chat and texted Ripley and Alexis. *New evidence! Get here as soon as you can!*

Ripley was the first to arrive. He slid his bike into Gilly's driveway, uprooting a freshly planted juniper and screeching to a stop inches from the garage. Alexis appeared a second later, a bag of pretzels clutched between her hand and handlebars. Gilly leapt from the porch and hurried over to join her friends.

"What's the big news?" asked Alexis. She straddled her bike and began tugging at a bag of pretzels.

"Guys, get this." Gilly leaned in like she was about to drop a gossip bomb. "Mrs. Cornthumper said her neighbor Judy saw a *suspicious* van in their neighborhood the day Thaddeus disappeared."

"Did it say *roto rooter*?" asked Ripley. "Because if it did, I'm officially off this case."

"No," Gilly gave him an annoyed look. "It was from a place that buys your junk."

"Props for granny," said Alexis through gritted teeth. She wrenched her hands back and forth—an epic battle between human and pretzel bag.

"Ugh, give me that," said Ripley, snatching the bag from Alexis. "You're such a bag novice. You have to squeeze it gently… let physics do the heavy lifting." He wrapped both hands around the bag and began to squeeze slowly.

"Do *not* crush my pretzels!" Alexis protested.

"Relax, your pretzels are fine; they're literally in a pillow of air." The words had barely left Ripley's lips when the bag exploded. Pieces of pretzel flew in every direction. Ripley handed the bag back to Alexis. "Opened."

Alexis clutched the bag to her chest, her mouth hanging open in disbelief. "Look what you did to my pretzels!"

"You can probably salvage some pieces

from your hair," comforted Gilly.

"Anyways," said Ripley, moving out of Alexis's reach. "You were saying Mrs. Cornthumper's neighbor saw a suspicious van."

"The van itself wasn't terribly suspicious; it's what was left behind when it pulled away."

"I'm guessing you're not going to say a cloud of exhaust," Ripley asked, scratching his nose.

"No," Gilly paused dramatically, "a blue feather."

"The van left a blue feather?" Ripley arched an eyebrow.

"It blew out the window onto the street. And before you ask, she did not see the driver and she did not get the license plate."

"Amateur," Ripley scowled. "You said the

van was white?" Gilly nodded enthusiastically. "Great, because there are only a *million* white vans out there. Should be easy to locate."

"Not with the words, *Your junk is our treasure*," Gilly grinned.

"Why didn't you lead with that?!" Ripley exclaimed. "We're wasting valuable time. We find that van, we find our thief!"

Chapter 7

Gilly ran upstairs, grabbed her laptop from her bedroom, raced willy-nilly down the stairs, and slid sock-footed into the kitchen. She joined Ripley at the table while Alexis rummaged through the kitchen cabinets.

"You have seven jars of peanut butter," Alexis nodded approvingly. "Respect."

"Help yourself," said Gilly.

"I think we should start with *Your junk is our treasure* and see what we find," suggested Ripley.

"Already on it." Gilly opened a browser and typed in the search string. "Hmm, seems to be a popular slogan. We have junkyards, trash collectors, Etsy, virtual marketplaces…" she continued to scroll down the webpage.

"Wait, what's that?" Ripley jabbed his finger at her screen.

"We buy your junk," read Gilly. She clicked the link. A hideous red and gold website loaded. "It's a pawn shop that buys gold."

"It's atrocious, is what it is," said Alexis, slurping down a Moo chocolate milk. "Their logo is an animated treasure chest." The three watched the screen, mesmerized by the pixelated treasure chest opening, spewing out golden coins, slamming shut, and then repeating.

"This website is archaic," said Ripley. "Was Mrs. Cornthumper sure it was a van and not a horse-drawn carriage?"

"Good one," Alexis snickered, fist-bumping him.

"There's the van," said Gilly, scrolling through the website. Alexis and Ripley leaned in to see.

"Alright, I've seen enough." Ripley pushed back from the table and stood as if he were about to lead a fighter squadron into war. "We need to get inside the pawn shop and rescue Thaddeus." He leapt from his chair and began to pace back and forth across the kitchen, "We'll need a distraction."

"A distraction?" asked Gilly.

"Yeah, think about it," Ripley explained. "They're not going to keep Thaddeus in their showroom. He's gonna be hidden from view, like in one of their offices."

"Got it," said Gilly. "We distract the owners while you search for Thaddeus."

"I'm thinking fireworks, or we set fire to something," suggested Alexis.

"Love the enthusiasm," said Ripley, "but I was thinking we could bring them something they'd want to buy. That way, we don't raise their suspicion."

"Eh," shrugged Alexis, "boring… but I see your point."

"I just hope Thaddeus is still there," said Gilly.

"Wait, why wouldn't he still be there?" asked Ripley, confused.

"You saw the condition of the boat," said Gilly. "What if they already found the treasure, and they no longer need Thaddeus?"

Ripley shook his head defiantly. "Thaddeus is fine. We made a promise to Mrs. Cornthumper, and I plan on keeping it."

Chapter 8

The trio coasted to a stop in front of Yum Fun Chinese Buffet. Marcel's Gold Emporium was across the street. The pawn shop's neon sign was weather-worn, and with the light for the *G* burned out, it read, Marcel's old Emporium, which Gilly declared was probably a more suiting name. The storefront was made up of floor-to-ceiling windows, covered with massive yellow strips of paper that offered: *Cash for Gold*, *Cash for Silver*, Antiques and *Jewelry 50% Off!*

 "Do you guys smell that?" Alexis smooshed her face against the window of the Chinese restaurant. "I'd like to make a proposal. A little *buffet action* before the pawn shop action?" She gave Ripley and Gilly a look of desperation. "This could be our last meal," she begged.

"We stick to the plan," said Ripley. "The sooner we get to Thaddeus, the better." He slung his scooter over his shoulder. "You guys hide your bikes, and we'll meet up at the front door in five."

"Food tyrant," mumbled Alexis as they wheeled their bikes away.

Gilly, the most detail-oriented of the group, devised *Operation Parrot Extraction*.

Ripley reluctantly accepted Gilly's mission's name over his name, *The

Parrot Squawks at Midnight. He, of course, thought hers was too literal.

Gilly's plan was to use the creepy porcelain doll that perched atop her bookshelf—its eyes followed you everywhere you went. Everywhere. Each night, before she went to sleep, she would turn the doll so it faced the opposite direction.

Her younger brother Brian liked to sneak into her bedroom as she slept and sit the doll on her nightstand so its topaz eyes stared into hers when she awoke. She returned her brother's thoughtfulness by coating his face in peanut butter while he slept and pulling the stopper on his ant farm. "Be free," she whispered.

While the girls hid their bikes, Ripley snuck along the side of the pawn shop. The parking lot was littered with trash and broken bottles. He double-checked to make sure no one was watching, slipped his scooter behind the dumpster, and hurried back to the front of the shop to rendezvous with the girls.

Alexis was aggressively chewing on something as they joined him.

"Emergency beef jerky," explained Gilly. Ripley gave an understanding nod.

A leather strip lined with bells *jingle jangled* as Ripley pushed the door open. Thick, stale air rushed up to meet them like a wet dog. Elevator jazz descended upon them from tiny circular speakers in the ceiling. The interior of the store looked like someone's attic had exploded. Sagging shelves held everything from artwork to a frightening ventriloquism dummy that gave Slappy vibes from the *Goosebumps* series.

"Look, your twin," Alexis pointed at the dummy dressed in a tuxedo.

"Look, your twin," Ripley retorted, pointing to a monkey with two cymbals.

"You two, knock it off," whispered Gilly.

The trio moved toward the rear of the store, where a long glass counter stretched along the entirety of the back wall, filled with baseball cards, comic books, coins, jewelry, and watches. A man shaped like an egg watched them approach with wary eyes.

"Can I help you?" He had the enthusiasm of an overripe banana.

"*May* I help you?" whispered Alexis.

Gilly gave Alexis the side eye as she approached the counter and shrugged off her backpack. "Good afternoon. I have to tell you, amazing store. So much, uhm… stuff."

"Uh-huh," the man grunted, fiddling with a watch band. He rolled his tongue on the inside of his cheek as he worked.

"I have small fingers," Gilly wiggled them in his face. "I can get that pin in there for you," she offered.

The man removed his glasses and gave Gilly a lackluster smile. "Go for it, kid." She snatched it up and within seconds, slid the spring-loaded pin into the side of the watch, attaching the band. "Thanks," grumbled the man.

"Sure, you'd do the same for me," Gilly smiled.

Gilly's favorite YouTube channel was *Tricks of The Mind*. It featured a psychologist who showed how easy it is to fool people's brains. She'd also learned that when you do something for someone, they feel obligated to do something for you in return. Reciprocity. She hoped that what she had learned would work in real life. So far, she had only practiced on her hamster.

"We're going to look around," said Ripley.

Gilly nodded and shooed them away. "My grandmother gave me this *really creepy* porcelain doll, and to be honest, it scares the heck out of me."

The man fought back a yawn and replied with an uninspired "Mhm."

Gilly continued, undeterred by the man's

lack of enthusiasm. "My grandmother said that it's been in the family for generations. The eyes are made out of something called blue topaz." She said the words *blue topaz* as if she had no idea what it was.

A tiny fire lit up behind the man's eyes. He scooched forward on his seat and rested his large, meaty arms on the counter. Gilly noticed his thumb was wrapped in a white bandage. "Name's Oliver, let's see what you got."

"I'm Gilly," she replied as she began unfastening the clasps that held the bag shut. She had Oliver's rapt attention.

While Gilly worked her distraction magic, Ripley and Alexis moved toward the hallway entrance at the far end of the counter.

"Now's your chance," whispered Alexis.

"Go!"

Ripley stole a quick glance over his shoulder, ducked out of sight, and scurried around the corner of the display case into the hallway. *Operation Parrot Extraction* was officially underway.

Chapter 9

Ripley froze in the hallway. A door, less than ten feet away, swung open with a *whoosh*. A lanky man with a ponytail and baggy overalls appeared. He hovered in the doorway for a moment, checked his phone, and then hurried down the hallway in the opposite direction, shouldering his way through a squeaky door that swung shut behind him.

Bathroom, guessed Ripley as he released a lungful of air and waited for his brain to relay a message to his heart that he was okay. He peeked into the room where the man had left and did a quick inventory. The man's office consisted of multiple towers of junk that created a narrow path leading to a battered metal desk. On the desk sat an ancient computer, keyboard, wallet, and a set of keys with a furry troll doll attached, but no sign of Thaddeus.

Alexis gave Gilly a discreet thumbs-up. Now, all she had to do was keep Oliver's attention while Ripley did his thing. She hoped her grandmother hadn't exaggerated when she told her that the doll was worth over two thousand dollars.

"This is a *beautiful* piece," said Oliver, admiring the doll. "I see that it was crafted in Germany."

"Yes, my great, great, great grandmother was from Munich," said Gilly.

Oliver's meaty fingers crawled across the counter and scooped up a jeweler's loupe. He held it up to his eye, making approving noises as he methodically examined the doll.

Ripley hurried to the next door, twisted the handle, and peered inside. It was filled with filing cabinets and printer paper—storage. His eyes swept the room; there was no sign of Thaddeus. A toilet flushed with a *woosh* just as he passed the bathroom.

The next door was an emergency exit, leaving only one door at the end of the hallway. *Bang!* The stall door slammed shut.

Hopefully, he's a stickler for hygiene! Ripley grabbed the doorknob of the last door and gave it a twist. Locked, of course. He eyed a fire extinguisher; he thought for a moment about smashing the lock. A squeaking noise came from the bathroom, knobs turning, and then the hissing sound of water.

"The keys!" whispered Ripley. He bolted down the hall, snatched the keys off the desk, and returned to the door. The ponytailed man began whistling. Ripley began sweating. He shoved the first key in the lock. It only went in about halfway and then got stuck. Ripley panicked and gave the keyring a hard tug. The keyring snapped in two, sending the troll doll and keys flying.

In the showroom, Gilly and Alexis watched all this play out on a black-and-white security camera video on a shelf behind Oliver.

Ripley crawled around on the floor, retrieving the keys. The *thrump, thrump* sound of the paper towel dispenser meant Ripley's time was up. He shoved another key in the lock and whispered a silent prayer. He twisted the doorknob, and the door swung open. He closed it behind him just in time.

"The doll seems to be in great condition. I'll give you four hundred dollars." Oliver gave her a toothy grin. "It's a bargain, believe me."

Gilly coughed. Alexis gasped. Not because of the low offer but because, at that very moment, Ripley appeared in the hallway, a covered birdcage swinging like a pendulum in front of him. He reared back and kicked open the emergency door, triggering a skull-pounding alarm.

"I'll have to think about it!" Gilly yanked the doll out of Oliver's hand. "Run!" The girls bolted through the store and into the blinding sunlight. Seconds later, Oliver was behind them. For a man his size, he could run.

"Come back here!" he screamed.

Cars honked and screeched as the girls zig-zagged between them. They crossed the street, grabbed their bikes, and leapt on them at a full run. Adrenaline pumped through their veins—they could hear

Oliver's footsteps pounding behind them. Alexis dared a glance over her shoulder, just in time to see Oliver hurl a trash can at them. A last-ditched effort of futility. He yelled a few choice words and then watched red-faced, eyes filled with anger, as they pedaled away. Now, they just had to make it to their rendezvous point and hope Ripley didn't get caught.

Luckily for Ripley, he'd slipped behind the dumpster, and ponytail man had sprinted right past him. He braced Thaddeus's cage between his legs, pressed the power button, and zoomed away. He lowered his sunglasses and smiled smugly as he raced along the busy street. He'd done it; he'd rescued Thaddeus.

Ten minutes later, Ripley pulled up beside Books For Less where the girls were waiting for him. "Come on!" he called out as he passed by. "Meet at Mrs. Cornthumper's!"

Chapter 10

Ripley beamed with pride as the others joined him at Mrs. Cornthumper's door. She was going to be so surprised. Alexis rang the doorbell. The three teens clustered together on the porch, looking like a clowder of Cheshire cats.

"You found Thaddeus!" exclaimed Mrs. Cornthumper, throwing open the door. "Yes, ma'am," smiled Ripley. He placed the cage onto her kitchen table and, like a magician, whooshed the cover off.

"Uhm… what's the matter with Thaddeus?" asked Gilly, slightly concerned.

"What did they do to him?" gasped Alexis, her hands flying to her face. Thaddeus stood stiff-legged and frozen to his perch.

"They stuffed him!" Gilly cried out in horror.

"Those monsters!" Alexis shook her fist.

"You three are going to be the death of me," declared Mrs. Cornthumper. "That's not Thaddeus—he's covered in dust and cobwebs." She collapsed into a chair. "That's not even his cage."

"Smooth move," Alexis complained.

Ripley didn't reply. He braced himself for what was sure to be an intense wailing session. Alexis was right—he'd messed up, big time. Mrs. Cornthumper's body began to shake. Ripley stared at his feet; he wished the ground would just open up and swallow him whole.

The dam finally broke. Mrs. Cornthumper howled with laughter.

Wait, what? Ripley was so confused.

"You stole someone's stuffed parrot! Tell me everything," she laughed through her tears.

Ripley was too stunned to speak. He stood quietly as Gilly and Alexis told their part of the story. "And then I look up," continued Gilly, "and there's Ripley, racing down the hallway with the cage."

"In my defense," said Ripley, finally finding his voice. "The storage room was pitch black. I saw the cage on the corner of a table, lifted the cloth, saw a parrot that looked like Thaddeus, and I took off."

"Oh my, I haven't laughed that hard since… well, since Cornelius was around." She looked at the teens and smiled. "Thank you." She eyed Ripley, "I guess we need to make things right and return the parrot to its proper owners."

Chapter 11

"I've never been so humiliated," sighed Ripley. He cruised along the sidewalk on his scooter toward the pawn shop. The parrot's cage rested between his legs, secured by a rubber strap.

"That's debatable," said Alexis under her breath.

"Don't be so hard on yourself. Any of us could have made that mistake," said Gilly.

Alexis arched a dubious eyebrow, "Speak for yourself."

"So, have you thought about what you're going to say?" asked Gilly.

"Here's your parrot back. I was going to feed him, but he's already stuffed." Alexis laughed so hard at her own joke she nearly crashed into a bush.

"I'm going to tell him the truth," Ripley smiled as Alexis rejoined them. "I'm going to tell them you stole the parrot, and I'm returning it."

"Can't wait to see how that goes," laughed Gilly.

The tingling bells didn't feel so tingly when the trio stepped into the pawn shop for the second time. Oliver looked a foot taller, and the ponytail man looked ready to play whac-a-mole with their heads. The two men scowled and crossed their arms in unison. Gilly had to wonder if they'd rehearsed.

"You're lucky your grandmother called," growled Oliver, pointing a stubby finger at Ripley. "We were about to call the police."

"Doubtful—" Gilly clamped her hand over Alexis's mouth, which wasn't the smartest move because she was known to eat just about anything. Alexis pried her lips free, "What? I was going to say that *most* pawn shops don't want police involved in their business."

"Kid's right," said the ponytail man. "Which means we like to take matters into our own hands." He cracked his knuckles and leaned forward onto the glass countertop. Ripley's eyes dropped to the man's hands. The words *your dead* were tattooed across his fingers. "Like my new tattoo?"

Ripley gulped and looked again; it was obvious he'd written the words with a sharpie. "I believe it's supposed to be *you're dead*, not *your dead*. I make that mistake all the time."

With the agility of an adolescent gazelle, the ponytail man leapt over the counter and grabbed Ripley by the front of his shirt. He lifted him off the ground, his feet dangling. "What did you say?"

"*Your* means something belongs to you!" Ripley cried out. "Like *your* parrot. You're means *you are.* Like, *you're* strong."

He tossed Ripley backward toward his friends, falling into Gilly's arms. Alexis raised an eyebrow.

"Listen," said Ripley in a falsetto, pushing Gilly's arms aside. "This was all a big misunderstanding. Please, if you would just let me explain."

"Oh, this is gonna be ripe, Marcel," said Oliver.

Ripley may not have known the difference between a live parrot and a stuffed parrot, but he could weave a masterful tale. By the time he'd finished his woeful tale about his grandmother—a.k.a. Mrs. Cornthumper—her lost love, and how she'd rescued hundreds of sea turtles off the coast of the Galapagos Islands only to be attacked and fight off a motley crew of Somalian pirates, the rugged pawn shop workers were reduced to tears.

"She's such a spectacular woman," sniffed Oliver.

"So you can understand," said Ripley, winding things up. "We were willing to risk *everything* to see our grandmother smile again." Marcel wiped his eyes with his sleeve. "We can't bring grandpa back… but we could rescue Thaddeus," Ripley let his shoulders slump and shook his head, "or so I tried."

Marcel crossed the room; his hands flew up to the front of Ripley's shirt. Ripley prepared himself to become a human projectile. Instead, Marcel gently straightened his shirt and looked him in the eye. "It took a lot of bravery to do what you did for your granny. I think we may have some information that can help you out."

"I-information?" Ripley stuttered. "You know where Thaddeus is?"

"I'm afraid not," said Marcel. "But I think I might know who does." He turned to Oliver, "Get the coin."

Chapter 12

"A man came in here a couple days ago and asked if we could authenticate a silver coin—"

"Did it have an eight stamped on it?" Gilly burst out. "Sorry," she apologized. "I got a little carried away. Please continue."

"I can see," Marcel laughed. "Yes, the coin was an authentic *pieces of eight*—probably dating back to the sixteenth, seventeenth century."

"That's so cool! Can we take a look?" asked Gilly.

"You're not going to bolt out the door with it, are you?" Marcel eyed her suspiciously.

Gilly's face turned bright red. "No," she apologized, "I'm really sorry about that."

Marcel handed her the coin, and Alexis and Ripley gathered around.

"It's heavier than I thought it would be," she said, feeling its weight in her palm. She handed it back to Marcel.

"Pristine condition, too," added Oliver. "We already have buyers interested in it."

"How much is it worth?" asked Alexis.

"About eight hundred dollars. I told him we'd give him five hundred," said Marcel.

A *ding* went off behind the counter. Oliver sauntered over to a microwave, removed a hot dog, tore open a ketchup packet, and squirted it the length of the hot dog. Alexis nearly went cross-eyed as the aroma wafted her way.

"You told him it was worth eight, and you'd give him five? Am I missing something?" asked Ripley.

"Not at all. It's the way pawn shops operate. We both make money, and the seller can remain anonymous," Oliver explained. "A lot of times, the items people bring to us aren't necessarily theirs to sell, if you catch my drift."

"We don't ask questions," clarified Marcel, sliding the coin back into a small plastic bag. "That's how we stay in business."

"So if the person doesn't volunteer any information—"

"We don't ask," said Oliver, finishing Ripley's sentence.

"Did this guy volunteer anything? Like where he found the coin or give you his name?" asked Ripley.

"Nope," said Marcel. "It was pretty obvious he was trying to remain incognito. Baseball cap, huge, mirrored sunglasses—you know the deal."

"He looked ridiculous," Oliver laughed.

"I got the impression that he had a lot more of the pieces of eight. He reassured us he'd be back," offered Marcel.

"So," Gilly frowned, "he's found grandma's treasure, and he's selling it off a little bit at a time."

"How old was he?" asked Alexis through

a mouthful of hot dog.

"Hey," complained Oliver, "get your filthy grubs off my food."

"Late sixties maybe," guessed Marcel. "He had that saggy neck thing going."

Alexis slipped her phone out of her pocket and surreptitiously dialed a number. The phone rang behind the counter. As Oliver turned to answer it, she expertly swiped another bite of his hot dog. When Oliver turned back around, Alexis pretended to be interested in an old, dusty book. He stared at his plate and then at Alexis.

"Well," Marcel clasped his hands together, "that's about all we've got for you. I've gotta get back to work. As you can see," he gestured toward his showroom, "business is booming."

"Of course," said Gilly, "you've been more than kind!"

"One more thing," Ripley piped up. "You said you thought the man had more coins." Marcel nodded. "If he comes back, can you call me? For my grandma," he added.

"Yeah, fine," Marcel sighed. "Oliver, hand

me a pad and pen."

Oliver nodded and made a rookie mistake. As soon as he turned, Alexis popped the hot dog out of the bun, squeezed the bun shut, and swallowed the hot dog with one gulp. She crossed the room and stood at the door, waiting for the others to join her.

Ripley scribbled his name and phone number onto the pad and handed it to Marcel. "Thanks again, guys!"

"Your name is Ripley?" laughed Marcel.

"Believe it or not," Ripley smiled.

"Alright. I'll call you if—" Marcel snapped

his fingers. "There is one other thing… it may be nothing."

"A lot of times, nothings turn into somethings," said Ripley.

"That man, when he came in, he put his phone on the counter. A text popped up on his screen… something like, *Cricket, you there?* He didn't text back, but he flipped his phone over. I messed with him, as I tend to do. Asked him if his first name was Jiminy."

"Oh," laughed Gilly, "like Jiminy Cricket."

"Yeah, I could tell he was annoyed," shrugged Marcel, "but he wanted information on the coin and the money."

"So he let it go," said Gilly.

"Yep. Like I said, it might be nothing, but it's a small town. Maybe someone will know him." He gave the trio a smile, and then waved them toward the door. "Now get out of here and stay out of trouble."

Oliver waved—munched down on his hot-dog-less hot dog, and realized he'd once again been bested by a thirteen-year-old. "Touché," he whispered. "Touché."

Chapter 13

"Are you sure?" asked Gilly. She sat on a park bench, trying to pry a piece of chewing gum off her shoe with a stick. She was sandwiched in between Ripley and Alexis, who at that very moment was thinking about a sandwich.

"Yes," Mrs. Cornthumper's earnest voice came through the phone speaker. "Otis 'Cricket' Mullins was that beastly man that accosted you at the marina. I tell you what, if I'd had my walking stick, I would have taught him a thing or two."

"I would have liked to have seen that," laughed Ripley.

"Please be careful. He's a buffoon, but he may also be a dangerous buffoon," she warned.

"We'll be careful, I promise." Gilly paused a moment. "We better get going; we need to follow up on the new clues."

"Alright," they could hear the hesitation and worry in her voice. "Bye, dears."

"Bye, Mrs. Cornthumper." Gilly hung up the phone, hopped up, and tossed the gum-prodding stick into a trash can. Ripley stretched and released a high-pitched yowl of a yawn.

"Somewhere, someone's windshield just cracked," said Alexis.

"We have a problem," said Gilly.

"Hey, speak for yourself," said Ripley.

"I am. Cricket knows who we are. There's no way he's going to let us go snooping around the marina," said Gilly.

"Pfft, can you see the disappointment on my face?" Ripley pointed at his face. "This is the face of disappointment."

"Is that what all the girls say?" Alexis teased.

Ripley rolled his eyes. "I have a plan." Alexis and Gilly exchanged worried glances. "What? When have my plans gone wrong?"

"The question should be, when have your plans gone right?" said Alexis. "You excel at failure."

"Do you want to hear my plan or not?"

"Fine," sighed Gilly. "We're listening."

Chapter 14

Operation Tall Woman

Gilly flung open the door, gathered her composure, and took a step forward, precariously balanced atop a pair of twelve-inch stilts hidden beneath a flowing yellow sundress. She grabbed the doorframe for a moment and then clomped into Cricket's office. He looked up at her from behind his cluttered desk and cocked his head to the side, a confused look on his face.

"Good day. Are you Cricket?" asked the tall blonde woman in a charming Southern voice. She brushed her hair from her face and pursed her lips.

"Yes, and you are…" Cricket's eyes flicked up and down as he took in the extraordinarily tall woman.

"Imogene. Imogene Flatbottom. We spoke on the phone an hour or so ago."

"Yes, of course. You were interested in the *Flaming Flamingo* pleasure craft."

"I am," she lowered her pink sunglasses and flashed a brilliant smile. "I understand the owner is out of town, but you said you could give me a tour?"

"I'd be happy to. Give me just a moment." Cricket opened a lockbox and removed a key attached to a puffy flamingo keychain. "After you," he gestured toward the door.

Gilly waited patiently outside for Cricket as he hung an Out of Office sign in the window, turned, and closed the door. She released a quiet sigh of relief. So far, *Operation Tall Woman* was working perfectly; Mr. Cricket seemed totally convinced that Mrs. Flatbottom was there to purchase a boat.

Operation Tall Woman was Ripley's idea, and thanks to Mika Mumford, a costume designer and makeup artist for the local theater, the plan went swimmingly. A blonde wig, a billowing yellow dress, a prosthetic nose, sunglasses, and a splendid array of costume jewelry and an hour of learning how to walk on twelve-inch stilts was all it had taken to transform Gilly from a thirteen-year-old girl into a towering, blonde Mrs. Flatbottom.

Alexis and Ripley hid behind the Edmond Tipps statue, listening to Cricket and Gilly's conversation on their phone. As soon as the harbor master was out of sight, Ripley and Alexis sprinted to his office. Alexis grabbed the door handle and gave it a tug. Even though it was locked, it swung open, thanks to an expertly placed wad of gum.

Ripley stepped into the office behind Alexis and took a quick look around. There was certainly nothing fancy about the room. A huge oak desk faced the door, and a computer, phone, notepad, and business card holder sat atop it. A detailed map of the harbor was affixed to the wall behind the desk, and beside that, an old gray file cabinet. An ancient air conditioner rattled in a window like chattering teeth.

Alexis snatched a candy bar off Cricket's desk, tore the wrapper off, and took a bite. "They are *so* right, Snickers is satisfying." She closed her eyes and moaned.

Ripley knew better than to chide her for eating while they snooped. Some of her best plans were pulled off during her snack attacks. "Well, Thaddeus isn't in here." The parrot's name had barely left his lips when they heard a weak *Squawk*. *Squawk*. Ripley froze.

Alexis stopped midchew—and that simply doesn't happen. "Did you hear that?" she whispered.

Ripley nodded and hurried across the room to a door with a gold placard that read, *Not a Public Restroom*. Ripley opened the door and flicked on the light switch, bathing them in harsh fluorescent light.

"Thaddeus," Alexis called out softly, taking a bite of her candy bar. She used the back of her hand and nudged the bathroom stall door open. A haggard, sickly-looking Thaddeus looked up at her from the bottom of his cage. "Oh, Thaddeus," her hand flew to her mouth.

"Pretty boy. Pretty boy," he squawked weakly.

"At least his eyes are okay," said Ripley, leaning into the stall beside Alexis.

Alexis smacked the back of his head. "Hi, pretty boy," she said softly. "Here," she unclasped the empty water tray from the cage and handed it to Ripley, "make yourself useful."

Ripley quickly filled the water tray and handed it back to Alexis. She fastened the water tray where Thaddeus could reach it. "He's so weak. I hope he's going to be okay."

"We've got to get him out of here," said Alexis, "before Cricket gets back."

"I'll text Gilly and let her know we found him." Ripley paused; a notebook on the back of the toilet caught his eye. He grabbed it and flipped it open. It was filled with handwritten notes and a card shaped like a heart. "Alexis, here's all of his notes and…."

"The card," Alexis whispered. She pulled her phone out and took a picture of Thaddeus.

"I'm pretty sure that's Thaddeus," said Ripley. "Plus, the heart-shaped card pretty much confirms it."

"I want to make sure we have the right parrot this time before I call Mrs. Cornthumper. I don't want to get her hopes up."

"No," Ripley agreed. "You're right."

"That won't be necessary," said a gruff voice. "Give me your phones."

Ripley startled—he knew that voice. Cricket stood in the doorway, an evil look on his face.

Chapter 15

"Where's Gilly?" demanded Ripley. Thaddeus rustled in the cage; he squawked and moved to the far side, trembling.

"She's a little tied up at the moment," Cricket smiled.

"You won't get away with this," sneered Alexis. She turned to the trembling parrot. "It's okay, Thaddeus," she said softly, "we've got this."

"Ha!" Cricket laughed aloud at Alexis's aplomb. "Give me your phones now!" he snarled. His face reddened like a thermometer that was about to pop.

"Alright," said Ripley, narrowing his eyes. "But I must warn you…" he tossed his phone in the air and caught it. The corner of Cricket's lip twitched as his eyes followed the phone.

"You're dealing with a *championship pitcher* from the Knights Softball League. I'm talking about a pitch cruising at your face like a guided missile at sixty miles per hour."

Before Cricket could respond, Ripley drew his arm back and launched his phone at the harbor master's head. It hurtled through the air toward him, whipping past his face, out the bathroom door, across the office, shattering the window, hitting the boardwalk, and skittering into the ocean. Everyone stood still for a moment.

"I hated that phone anyways."

"You idiot!" Cricket trembled with rage.

"And you call yourself a pitcher. Pitiful," he growled.

"Actually, I wasn't talking about me." Ripley shifted to the side; Alexis's arm spun like a windmill on caffeine. She launched her phone, sending it spinning end over end like a ninja-throwing star—it thwacked Cricket right between the eyes. He released a high-pitched yelp, said something about taking his coffee black, and then crumbled to the ground unconscious.

"Sheesh, that was *brilliant*!" Ripley exclaimed. "Frightening… but brilliant."

"Let's get out of here before he wakes up!" Alexis handed Ripley the spiral notebook and then knelt in front of Thaddeus's cage. "You're gonna be just fine," she cooed. "I promise."

"Pretty boy," rasped Thaddeus. He was still trembling with fright.

They half-stepped, half-leapt over Cricket

into his office. Alexis gently placed the birdcage on the desk and retrieved her phone from the floor beside the collapsed man.

"What do we do with him?" asked Ripley. As if on cue, Cricket's eyelids fluttered, and he began to moan.

"Bathroom," suggested Alexis. "We need to hurry though; he's coming to."

Alexis and Ripley each took a leg and hauled him through the door into the bathroom. Ripley knelt and removed Cricket's shoes and socks and tossed them in the toilet. "Hey, what did one toilet say to the other?" Alexis gave him a quit-messing-around look. "Quit stalling!" laughed Ripley. "Get it? Stalling."

"I thought you were gonna say you looked flushed," Alexis replied.

The two teens hurried back into the office. Alexis placed Thaddeus by the front door while Ripley shoved Cricket's desk in front of the bathroom door. Together, they added a lamp, a chair, and then toppled a file cabinet to the pile. "That should hold him for a bit," said Ripley, wiping his brow.

Alexis grabbed Thaddeus and opened the

door. The sun sparkling off the water was blinding. Ripley stepped out behind her and lowered his sunglasses. "Why did you throw his shoes and socks in the toilet?"

"I'm hoping he has tender little baby feet so he can't chase us."

"Hm," nodded Alexis, "makes sense."

"Alright, call Mrs. Cornthumper and get Thaddeus to safety. I'm going to try to find Gilly," said Ripley.

"You know where she is?" asked Alexis.

"My money's on the *Flaming Flamingo*," Ripley replied, scanning the marina. He turned to Alexis, "You've gotta go!"

"Okay," she gave a quick nod. "Good luck!"

Chapter 16

Ripley ran along the main walkway. He had a pretty good idea where the boat was located since he and Alexis had watched Cricket and Gilly from behind the statue. It took him less than a minute to spot the hot pink *Flaming Flamingo*. He sprinted to her slip and then leapt from the dock onto the boat. He ran down a short flight of steps to the cabin. The door was locked.

"Gilly, are you in there?!" Ripley put his ear to the door; he could hear muffled noises coming from inside. "Stand back I'm going to kick the door open!"

Ripley took a step back. He'd seen dozens of movies and TV shows where the hero kicked the door open. Now, it was his moment to shine. He threw up his leg and slammed his foot into the door.

The impact was jarring; there was a loud crunching sound. Only, it wasn't the door. His eyes rolled up in their sockets, and he moaned and fell backward, still feeling the violent vibration reverberating through his body.

He lay on the steps for a few moments, staring at the clouds, wondering if he'd ever walk again. He released a long, slow rush of air and struggled to his feet. In his peripheral vision, he saw a very angry, barefoot Cricket emerge from the office. "You gotta be kidding me."

Ripley knew there was no way he could kick that door open. He began digging through storage bins, lockers, fishing equipment, and then he spotted it, a fire extinguisher. Finally, he'd get to test his theory! He grabbed it, ran down the stairs, and slammed it feverishly against the door. Finally, the lock gave, and the door flew open.

"Gilly!" Ripley cried out. He rushed over to his friend and ripped the duct tape off her mouth.

"Ouch, you nut job!" She teetered on her stilts.

"Hey, a little thanks would do." He pulled out his pocket knife, spun Gilly around by the shoulders, and cut through the tape. Gilly smacked him on the back of the head. "I deserved that," Ripley grimaced.

Gilly began pulling at her stilts when Ripley stopped her. "Cricket's coming, no time for that."

They both felt a heavy *thud* and then the rocking of the boat. Their hearts sank in unison—Cricket was onboard.

"Never mind," Ripley exhaled, "the behemoth hath arriveth."

Gilly and Ripley clambered up to the main deck. Gilly held her hand to her eyes, protecting them from the sun. "What happened to him?" she whispered. Cricket's forehead and nose were red and swollen.

"He missed a call," whispered Ripley.

Cricket pointed a flare gun at them. "Get in the cabin now!" He stomped his bare foot in anger.

"Oar…" said Ripley, extending the word oar.

Cricket gave Ripley a look that would have melted titanium. "Get in the cabin, now." Gilly teetered on her stilts on the rocking boat.

"Oar…" Ripley taunted.

The air whistled and then resounded with a loud thwack and for the second time that day, Cricket crumbled to the ground unconscious. Mrs. Cornthumper stood behind him, brandishing an oar.

"I tried to warn him," shrugged Ripley.

Chapter 17

Gilly plodded into Mrs. Cornthumper's kitchen. She seemed to have embraced her stilts, and the fact that everyone had to look up to her wasn't so bad either.

"Well," Alexis rummaged through the refrigerator, "at least I know what to get you for your birthday."

"She kind of reminds me of Grover from *Percy Jackson*," Ripley observed. He plucked a grape from a bowl on the kitchen table and handed it to Thaddeus who gripped it in his claw. "It shouldn't be too hard to figure out what song we're looking for, Mrs. Cornthumper; you're like, what, a hundred years old?"

"Watch it," Mrs. Cornthumper thumped her fist into her hand, "you've seen what I can do with an oar."

"It's just," Ripley moved, putting the table in between him and Mrs. Cornthumper. "Did they even have music back then?" Gilly shot Ripley a warning look.

"Ignore him, Mrs. Cornthumper. Ripley gets a little cocky when he solves a case," said Gilly.

"It's not completely solved," said Alexis. "There's still treasure unaccounted for."

"That's right," said Gilly. "Cricket admitted everything to the police. He never found the treasure. Only a few coins Cornelius had hidden on the boat."

"That's why he tore the boat apart," said Ripley.

"Pretty boy, *squawk*," belted out Thaddeus.

"Yes, you are," said Mrs. Cornthumper, lovingly stroking the parrot's head. She reached for another grape, only to realize the bowl was empty. Alexis stood a few feet away, innocently staring out the kitchen window, her cheeks puffed out like a chipmunk.

"You said to find the key to your husband's puzzle, we needed to figure out the first song you two danced, too."

"Yes, to figure out what the cipher is," nodded Mrs. Cornthumper.

"You met Cornelius when you were sixteen? Is that right?" Gilly asked.

"Yes."

"And you had your first dance at seventeen?" Gilly continued.

"I had just turned seventeen. We went to Baron's Soda Shop. *That* I remember." A huge smile crossed her face, "And we both had banana splits; only he had his without the banana." She shook her head, "He was so silly."

"Why didn't he have a banana?" asked Gilly.

"He said it had split," Mrs. Cornthumper shook her head. "He was filled with horrible puns."

"Sorry to interrupt, but where do you keep… ah!" Alexis exclaimed, banging a cabinet door shut. "Never mind, found it."

"What on *earth* are you doing, child?"

All heads turned toward Alexis. Flour, milk, sugar, and eggs lined the counter like toy soldiers. "Go ahead," she insisted, stirring the ingredients into a large mixing bowl. "I'm listening. Not sure how long this is going to take." She jabbed a finger at the oven a few times, setting it to preheat, leaving a circle of flour on each button. Mrs. Cornthumper's mouth moved, but no words came out.

"Ahem," said Gilly, getting everyone's attention. "I've created a list of the top twenty songs from the 1950s. I'm guessing it's going to be one of them."

"Do you remember if it was a slow song or a fast song?" asked Ripley.

"What he's really asking is if it was a *romantic*, *slowwww* dance," Alexis teased, licking the batter off the whisker. Ripley's face turned bright red.

Mrs. Cornthumper closed her eyes, her face becoming serene as a slight smile tickled her lips. "It was fast," she nodded. I can still see him swinging me around, laughing." Her smile became broader.

"Sure he wasn't trying to escape?" teased

Ripley.

"Shh! Stay in the moment," urged Gilly, pulling her phone out of her pocket. "I'm going to read you the songs that I found from when you were seventeen." She tapped the screen and opened her Notes app. "Okay, 'Rock Around the Clock,' 'Tutti Frutti,' 'Hound Dog.'"

Gilly paused for a moment. Mrs. Cornthumper shook her head, "None of those, dear."

"Alright, I've got a bunch more," Gilly continued. "'That'll Be the Day,' 'Heart Break Hotel,' 'Johnny B. Good,'" everyone jumped when Thaddeus squawked.

"*Grouchiest!*" Thaddeus bobbed his head and shuffled along his perch.

"Did he just say grouchiest?" asked Alexis, sliding a pan into the oven and closing the door with her foot.

"Mrs. Cornthumper," Gilly looked with excitement, "Does the song 'Johnny B. Good'—"

"Grouchiest!" Thaddeus belted out again.

"—ring any bells?" Gilly laughed. Mrs. Cornthumper didn't have to answer; a huge smile had filled her face.

"I remember," she squealed with delight. "I remember!"

Chapter 18

Ripley flipped Cricket's notebook open. Page after page was filled with scribbles and doodles where the harbor master had tried to solve the puzzle Cornelius had left for his wife. Ripley removed the heart-shaped card from the envelope and placed it on the kitchen table. Gilly, Alexis, and Mrs. Cornthumper drew closer as he read the clue aloud.

"To my better half. The treasure we searched for over twenty years is: *3_ _ 7 1*9 5 7 *_ 6 7 4 7 8 *2 _ *7 6 0 5 9. I love you! Cornelius."

"Thanks to Thaddeus," Gilly smiled sweetly at the parrot, "we know that the word *grouchiest* is the cipher key." She pointed to a whiteboard attached to the pantry door. "Do you mind?"

"Not at all." Mrs. Cornthumper picked up the eraser and wiped the board.

Gilly picked up the clue and copied it onto the whiteboard with a black marker. Then, using a red dry erase marker she wrote the word *grouchiest* below the cryptic message. Everyone huddled around the pantry.

"It's going to be a simple substitution cipher," said Alexis. "Where each number corresponds to a letter in the alphabet."

"Yep, but instead of using the whole alphabet," said Ripley, "we're just going to use each of the letters in *grouchiest*."

"May I make a suggestion?" Mrs. Cornthumper piped in. "Cornelius and I used to solve puzzles like this all the time. I would start by *simplifying* the clue."

"I'm all ears," said Gilly, rolling the pen back and forth between her thumb and index finger.

"What are the most commonly used letters in the alphabet?" asked Mrs. Cornthumper.

"I know the letter E is one of them," offered Ripley.

Gilly whipped out her bedazzled phone and quickly performed a search. "The top five letters are E, T, A, O, I.”

“And grouchiest has *three* of the five letters,” said Alexis excitedly.

“Alright,” said Gilly. “If we look at the code, the number seven is used the most.” She used her thumb to erase the sevens off the whiteboard and replaced them with the letter E.

*3 - - e 1*9 5 e * - 6 e 4 e 8 *2 - *e 6 0 5 9

“I'm guessing the asterisks are there to separate the words?” Ripley asked. “So we can remove those?”

"Exactly," praised Mrs. Cornthumper.

"I've done a bit of cryptology," Ripley bragged. He made a fist and blew across his knuckles.

"Oh, brother," Gilly rolled her eyes and smudged away the asterisks with her thumb. "That leaves us with…"

3 - - e 1 9 5 e - 6 e 4 e 8 2 - e 6 0 5 9

"So the puzzle is five words." Alexis stuck out her bottom lip and pinched it between her finger and thumb. "The second word is three letters, and we're guessing it ends in E."

"Which would most likely be the word *the*," said Ripley, finishing her thought. "Replace the nines with a T and the fives with an H."

Gilly used her thumb again as a magic eraser and then scribbled in the new letters. The puzzle now read:

3 - - e 1 t h e - 6 e 4 e 8 2 - e 6 0 h t

"I feel like we're on that game show, *Wheel of Fortune*," said Gilly.

"Yeah, you just spin a wheel and call out a letter," laughed Ripley. "All we need is Vanna White."

"Guys," Alexis began tapping the whiteboard with her index finger. "There's only five words, according to Google that start with E and end with an H and a T. *Eight*! The last word is *Eight*!"

"Brilliant! So, we replace the sixes with I's and the number 0 with a G."

3 - - e 1 t h e - 6 e 4 e 8 2 - e i g h t

"Alexis," Ripley gasped, "you're a genius."

"Déjà vu," whispered Alexis.

"Let's see how it lines up with our cipher," said Gilly. "We know that nine is T. Seven is E, and five is H." She wrote the numbers under the letters.

"Six is I," said Ripley, "and zero is G."

G R O U C H I E S T

0 5 6 7 9

"It goes in order!" said Alexis excitedly. She snatched the pen from Gilly and scribbled the remaining numbers beneath the word. In a matter of seconds, they'd solved the puzzle.

G R O U C H I E S T

0 1 2 3 4 5 6 7 8 9

"Under the pieces of eight," gasped Ripley. "It's under your boat!"

3_EITHE_6E4E82_EIGHT
GROUCHIEST
0 1 2 3 4 5 6 7 8 9

Chapter 19

Ripley, Alexis, and Gilly burst through the water's surface. Ripley tore his mask off and spat out his snorkel in a glorious eruption of spittle and salt water.

"We found it!" he shouted, gulping in a mouthful of water. "We found it!"

Mrs. Cornthumper leaned over the side of

the boat and steadied the weighted ladder as the teens clambered aboard. Pools of water puddled around their bare feet. "You actually found it," her eyes were filled with wonderment as if it were too good to be true.

"It was there all along," said Gilly breathlessly. "Cornelius hid the rope beneath the boat's motors so no one would see it."

"I can't believe it," said Mrs. Cornthumper breathlessly.

"Well, believe it," smiled Alexis, taking a bite of seaweed she'd somehow acquired on her dive. Ripley hurried over to the twin Yamaha engines, leaving behind a trail of wet footprints. A thick, braided, nylon rope was cleverly hidden just below the engine housing. He gripped the rope with both hands and tugged—it barely moved. "It's crazy heavy!" he yelled over his shoulder. "Give me a hand!"

Alexis took one bite and chucked her seaweed overboard. Then, she and Gilly shouldered in on either side of Ripley and took hold of the slick rope.

"Pull together on three," instructed Gilly. "One, two, three, pull! One, two, three, pull!"

"It's too heavy," said Ripley. "The one day I skip my protein shake."

"It's close to a thousand pounds," said Alexis. "Plus it's waterlogged."

"I have an idea," said Mrs. Cornthumper. And without another word, she hurried across the boat.

"I hate it when people do that," Ripley's shoulders sagged. "They say they have an idea, and then they run away."

"I know, are we supposed to follow them? Or are we mere observers in this *sinister* game?"

"What?" Ripley gave Alexis a confused look.

"Line from a movie," Alexis shrugged, "but you have to admit it fit."

Teetering from side to side without her walking stick, Mrs. Cornthumper returned carrying a huge chunk of circular metal that resembled a massive fishing rod. "It's a winch. With a little creativity, we should be able to make it work!"

"Gilly, you're up," said Ripley. "She assembled a working drawbridge from a carton of milk, tongue depressor, some ChapStick and a staple gun."

Gilly took the winch from Mrs. Cornthumper and gave it a once-over. She nodded her head and shooed everyone away. "I need room to work. Ripley, you're in my light."

"There's literally sunlight everywh—" Gilly gave him an icy stare, which wasn't easy on a sunny day. "Fine. Fine." Ripley backed away. "You're right."

For the next few moments there was only grunts and groans, then, "Scalpel!" Gilly held out her hand like a surgeon, expecting to be handed a surgical tool.

Ripley hurried over and plopped his pocket knife into her hand. Gilly shooed him away again.

Alexis, Mrs. Cornthumper and Ripley watched in anxious silence. A pelican had even alighted atop a barnacle-covered pole to watch.

"It's ready!" Gilly cried out dramatically, throwing her arm to her forehead, wiping away the nonexistent sweat. "I need a cookie. Stat!" She had secured the winch to the boat and knotted the rope inside the drum. She began to turn the crank arm, the back of the boat dipped downward, bobbing under the weight. Ripley hurried over and helped. This time Gilly didn't chase him away.

It felt an eternity, but then, amidst a cloud of bubbles and debris, the top of a thick canvas bag emerged into view. A few more cranks, and together, they hoisted the bag up level with the side of the boat.

"We've either got treasure or someone's trash," said Ripley.

Mrs. Cornthumper was overcome with emotion. She and her husband had searched for this treasure for years, decades, and now here it was. Cornelius had found it, and together, with her new friends, they had solved his last puzzle.

It took some ingenuity and patience, but together they were able to secure the cocoon-like bag to the back of the boat with rope and duct tape.

"Here, Mrs. Cornthumper." Ripley handed her his trusty pocket knife.

Mrs. Cornthumper stood and thought for a moment; to her, this moment meant the beginning and the end. A smile crossed her face as she slit the top of the bag open, revealing a sea of silver coins glistening brilliantly in the sunlight.

Ripley turned to his friends and smiled. They had done it. Thaddeus was home safe. They'd solved Cornelius's puzzle and found the treasure. And they had made Mrs. Cornthumper a very happy, very rich woman.

She reached out and pulled the teens into a tight hug.

"Thank you," she whispered. "Thank you."

"Now, about renegotiating our contract," squeaked Ripley.

Thank you for reading
The Parrot Squawks at Midnight

Sign up for the latest info on upcoming books, bonus content, and giveaways at:

twistedkeypublishing.com/TL

I hope you enjoyed reading the first book in the *Ripley Kool and the Investigator* series. Please leave a review on Amazon, Goodreads, or Barnes & Noble. I'd love to hear from you! The second book in the series is *The Vanishing Raptor*.

Be sure to follow me on Amazon,

Goodreads, or sign up for my newsletter to receive notifications on my new releases:

twistedkeypublishing.com/TL

Others by Thomas Lockhaven

Ava & Carol Detective Agency

Join Ava and Carol, two clever detectives, on a thrilling journey through ancient treasures, daring chases, and unexpected alliances. *The Mystery of the Pharaoh's Diamonds* will leave young readers spellbound!